Vessels of Honour
Ready for the Master's use

Dr Michael Andam

Vessels of Honour
Ready for the Master's use

KDP

Vessels of Honour: Ready for the Master's use
© 2020 Dr. Michael Andam

Published by KDP

Dedicated to
All followers of Jesus Christ

Content.

Preface

Over the last twenty years, I have heard many statements made in various churches and on media networks. Many are biblical and unfortunately majority is not from the Bible. There are many in churches that follow after heretics and stand to defend such unbiblical doctrines. There are many going round as of today.

For this study, we will be looking at how important the hearts of individuals are to God. The reason I felt the need to respond to this is how some leaders of some churches have made their congregation believe in certain doctrines. There is a word many have used which I believe have put them on pedestals. They call themselves 'anointed men or women of God' and thus untouchable and accountable to no one in their church especially when they are the 'founders.' You hear some of their church members talking about how their pastors are anointed. The word anointing in the Old Testament simply means to smear with oil. In the New Testament, God has made salvation open to all as in John 1:12.

God is able to use anyone who makes himself or herself available for the Master's work. True ministers of the gospel are a gift of God to the church and are to be respected and not worshipped. This study looks at how every child of God bought with the blood of Jesus can be used mightily just as those in the New Testament. Jesus sent the seventy because their hearts were ready to be used by the Lord. The Bible did not name them as pastors or leaders.

This study is aimed at challenging Christians who want to see God's power in demonstration in their lives. It has all to do with our heart and willingness to obey and do God's Word.

1 Hidden hearts?

God knows you

When we talk about the heart, or our spirit man, there is only one person who knows us very well. God relates with us through our spirit. He is God Almighty the Creator of man and everything in the universe. Our heart is the operating center of both our physical and spiritual life. It is like the central processing unit of a computers (CPU). The heart works with the mind to make decisions and execute actions.

We can go about pretending to be what we are not to deceive people or to create some false impressions, but God sees everything. God who dwells in light sees everyone and everything whether in light or darkness. He knows those whose hearts are towards Him to obey and do His will. This is how the apostle Paul explains it:

"Nevertheless the solid foundation of God stands, having this seal: "The Lord knows those who are His," and, "Let everyone who names the name of Christ depart from iniquity.""-II Timothy 2:19.

The question is this, are you one of God's children? This is something we need to consider seriously as a matter of urgency. It does not matter what you have done, your background or sins you have and still committing. The call of Jesus Christ to you is still the same, "Come to Me, all you who labor and are heavy laden, and I will give you rest."-Matthew 11:28.

We are to have a practical knowledge of who God is through daily experience. We cannot go through the Christian life with ignorance and simply quoting scriptures and going through the motions.

The payment of sin, conquering the enemy and making a public display of them is not hidden. On the cross Jesus finished the work of redemption and reconciliation. He was the Passover lamb slain for all once and for all. Anyone who receive Jesus' free gift of eternal life becomes a child of God. John explains it as follows: "But as many as received Him, to them He gave the right to become children of God, to those who believe in His name: who were born, not of blood, nor of the will of the flesh, nor of the will of man, but of God."-John 1:12-13.

Each and every one of us has been given a gift called free will. God gave that to Adam and Eve and all their descendants including us today. With this we are able to make choices. This is the reason why God never forces anyone to accept the free gift of life offered in Christ Jesus as mentioned earlier. He has made an open invitation and it is up to us to accept or reject with the attached ramifications.

God sees all-Heart and mind
"Every way of a man is right in his own eyes, but the LORD weighs the hearts."-Proverbs 21:2
God sees everyone and all our ways are open before Him. Although men may see things right in their own judgment, God weighs every heart. This simply means all our motives; desires and plans are transparent before God. He sees everything in our heart.

There was a time God sent His prophet Samuel to anoint the second king for Israel. God sent him to the house of a man called Jesse. When the first born of Jesse stood before the prophet, he thought from his stature, this was indeed the chosen one. "So it was, when they came, that he looked at Eliab and said, "Surely the LORD's anointed is before Him!""-I Samuel 16:6.

God had a different way of assessing this. This was what he told the prophet:

"But the LORD said to Samuel, "Do not look at his appearance or at his physical stature, because I have refused him. For the LORD does not see as man sees; for man looks at the outward appearance, but the LORD looks at the heart.""-I Samuel 16:7.

God uses the criteria of looking at the heart to access us. He said He had rejected the one the prophet thought had the right physical stature fit to be a king. The prophet Jeremiah gave us an insight into how God operate using this concept. "I, the LORD, search the heart, I test the mind, even to give every man according to his ways, according to the fruit of his doings."-Jeremiah 17:10.

God made it known that it is He, the Lord Who searches the heart and test the mind. This is an indication of how important our spiritual life is. The heart and mind are part of our spiritual life when it comes to God. As mentioned earlier, it is linked to both our physical and spiritual life. If we want to please the Lord Jesus Christ, it has to be done from the heart and linked with the mind. It is such a privilege for us to be given God's criterion for assessing us.

The apostle Peter defending the coming of the Spirit upon all including what was described as the gentiles stated that it is God who knows the heart. "So God, who knows the heart, acknowledged them by giving them the Holy Spirit, just as He did to us,"-Acts 15:8.

Vessels in the house

The Bible teaches on the subject of having various types of vessels in a great house. I believe this this is true for any other home as well. These vessels will not be literal but our hearts that are ready for kingdom work.

"But in a great house there are not only vessels of gold and silver, but also of wood and clay, some for honour and some for dishonour. Therefore if anyone cleanses himself from the latter, he will be a vessel for honour, sanctified and useful for the Master, prepared for every good work."-II Timothy 2:20-21.

I remember growing up as a child in my parents' home; we had various types of drinking glasses. We had the ones used daily by everyone. There were some with 'gold' finish kept in a cabinet. We were not allowed to go near them. You dare to take any from the cabinet unauthorised! These were used to serve very important quest that visited my parents. There were others such as wine glasses, although none drank alcohol in the family.

When we were young our cups were made of plastic! It was gradually upgraded when we grew up into maturity and were more capable of handling glasses.

When my dad came home and was thirsty, he would use the available clean cup to drink water. It did not matter if it was plastic or ordinary glass. He did not go to the special cabinet to take one of the golden-rimmed glasses.

This could explain that if anyone cleanses himself or herself by allowing the word of Christ to transform them, they could become vessels of honour in God's great house. We could be useful for our Master for every good work.

2 After God's Heart

Who is he?

There was a man God described as after God's heart. Even before this man was aware how God saw him, something extraordinary was about to happen to him. His life was about to be changed forever. History and all generations were about to talk about him always for thousands of years to come. In fact God was going to use him as a measurement of how good or evil kings who reigned in Israel were rated!

The apostle Paul testified of this as part of Israel's history when he preached to a group of people ready for the word of Christ. "And when He had removed him, He raised up for them David as king, to whom also He gave testimony and said, 'I have found David the son of Jesse, a man after My own heart, who will do all My will.'"-Acts 13:22. Seeking after God's heart means the willingness to do God's will. It is as simple as that and God sees that.

David's story was very interesting. He was chosen by God and anointed as king while the incumbent king was still alive for a period of years. The first king of Israel found it difficult to follow and obey God's instructions for His people. God rejected him as his heart was turned away from God. "Now the LORD said to Samuel, "How long will you mourn for Saul, seeing I have rejected him from reigning over Israel? Fill your horn with oil, and go; I am sending you to Jesse the Bethlehemite. For I have provided Myself a king among his sons.""-I Samuel 16:1.

Ready to be used

A heart ready will not go unnoticed by God. The Messiah Jesus had to come from David's lineage. "From this man's seed, according to the promise, God raised up for Israel a Savior—Jesus—"-Acts 13:23.

It would be great to have a guide on how we can get our hearts right in living our life to be pleasing to God. David's life will be a good guide for us to learn and practice. It would be like what is known in the corporate business world as a roadmap to guide us.

How was his heart for God?

There are several versus in David's own writings in the book of psalms that reveals his heart towards God. We will look at some of these. We will also group them into various subheadings to help with our practice. The following writings give us some idea what kind of attitude God looks for in our heart.

- ⊙ **Love:** David loved the Lord. "I will love You, O LORD, my strength."-Psalms 18:1. One is likely to obey the will of God there when there is an absolute demonstration of love for Him. Jesus said if you love Him then you will obey His commandments. Love and obedience go hand in hand.

- **Reverence:** David's reverence of God was remarkable. "I will call upon the LORD, who is worthy to be praised; So shall I be saved from my enemies."-Psalms 18:3. Throughout the book of psalms, David is full of reverence to God just as this writing.

- **Obedient:** "Give me understanding, and I shall keep Your law; Indeed, I shall observe it with my whole heart."-Psalms 119:34. David did not just pretend to desire understanding of God's Word to obey them. He practised them consistently. He was going to observe His law with his whole heart. There was no partiality when it came to obedience to God for David.

- **Trust:** There is not anyone who wrote about trusting in the Lord than David. He practiced this and wrote a great deal about his experiences. "The LORD is my light and my salvation; Whom shall I fear? The LORD is the strength of my life; Of whom shall I be afraid? -Psalms 27:1. "To You, O LORD, I lift up my soul. O my God, I trust in You; Let me not be ashamed; Let not my enemies triumph over me."-Psalms 25:1-2. In the popular psalm of David, he makes a declaration of absolute trust in God His Shepherd. "Yea, though I walk through the valley of the shadow of death, I will fear no evil; For You are with me; Your rod and Your staff, they comfort me."-Psalms 23:4.

- **Respect:** "Have mercy on me, O LORD, for I am in trouble; my eye wastes away with grief, yes, my soul and my body!"-Psalms 31:9. David was not proud before his God. He respected God enough to come to Him for help when in trouble.

- **Fear of God:** "Establish Your word to Your servant, who is devoted to fearing You."-Psalms 119:38. David feared God. Because of that He asked the Lord to establish His word to him. That is a key for us to note. Having the word of God will keep us from drifting away from God.

- **Humility:** "Surely men of low degree are a vapor, men of high degree are a lie; If they are weighed on the scales, they are altogether lighter than vapor. -Psalms 62:9. David acknowledged that we are nothing no matter what we have or do. He compared both degrees of men and arrived at the same conclusion. We are together lighter than vapour which would disappear without a trace. "The humble He guides in justice, and the humble He teaches His way."-Psalms 25:9.

- **Faithful and devoted:** "Surely goodness and mercy shall follow me all the days of my life;

and I will dwell in the house of the LORD Forever."-Psalms 23:6. David was faithful and devoted his life serving and obeying God at all times. His desire was to dwell in the house of God forever and that implies experiencing His presence.

- **Repentant:** "For Your name's sake, O LORD, pardon my iniquity, for it is great."-Psalms 25:11. "Against You, You only, have I sinned, and done this evil in Your sight— That You may be found just when You speak, and blameless when You judge."-Psalms 51:4. David was quick to acknowledge his sins and repent immediately. "The sacrifices of God are a broken spirit, A broken and a contrite heart— These, O God, You will not despise."-Psalms 51:17.

3 Channel of blessings

Blessings for families

When God was looking for a channel to direct His blessings to families of the world, He had to find one with a heart towards Him. He found Abraham. God does not choose the qualified. His standards are so high no one will meet it. In view of this, He calls us and then qualifies us. In between is the series of tests to know what is in our hearts. The good news is that once God find the qualities we saw listed for David, it could mean our hearts are right for Him to use.

Chosen vessel

"Now the LORD had said to Abram: "Get out of your country, from your family and from your father's house, to a land that I will show you. I will make you a great nation; I will bless you and make your name great; and you shall be a blessing. I will bless those who bless you, and I will curse him who curses you; and in you all the families of the earth shall be blessed.""Genesis 12:1-3.

This was God's plan for Abraham. In reality, God had examined Abraham's heart and tested his mind to choose him for this task. Other than that,

God will not have visited and spoken to him with regards to moving to where He God would show him.

Obedience to call

"So Abram departed as the LORD had spoken to him, and Lot went with him. And Abram was seventy-five years old when he departed from Haran."-Genesis 12:4. The first part of this shows that Abraham had a heart of obedience. He departed immediately leaving the comfort of his environment and comfort zone.

Series of Tests

With Abraham, God had to use a series of tests to get to know his heart even more. The greater the task the more God will test our hearts to match the level of task. It started with the promise to have a child in a human impossible circumstance.

"After these things the word of the LORD came to Abram in a vision, saying, "Do not be afraid, Abram. I am your shield, your exceedingly great reward." But Abram said, "Lord GOD, what will You give me, seeing I go childless, and the heir of my house is Eliezer of Damascus?""-Genesis 15:1-2.

Abraham reminded God that he had no child to fulfil this promise. He rather presented an alternative to God. God rejected this, as it was not part of His plan. God took him outside to show Abraham what his future descendants He was promising will look like. "And behold, the word of the LORD came to him, saying, "This one shall not be your heir, but one who will come from your own body shall be your heir." Then He brought him outside and said, "Look now toward heaven, and count the stars if you are able to number them." And He said to him, "So shall your descendants be." And he believed in the LORD, and He accounted it to him for righteousness."-Genesis 15:4-6.

The lesson here is that we cannot impress God with our perceived limitations. His plan and purpose go beyond our ability to accomplish anything alone. That is why it is His plan for you. He is to assist you with His supernatural power to accomplish it.

Visitation

The series of test carried on. When God's time was near to fulfil the promise of the covenant child for Abraham and Sarah, He went to visit them Himself.

"Then the LORD appeared to him by the terebinth trees of Mamre, as he was sitting in the tent door in the heat of the day. So he lifted his eyes and looked, and behold, three men were standing by him; and when he saw them, he ran from the tent door to meet them, and bowed himself to the ground,...Then they said to him, "Where is Sarah your wife?" So he said, "Here, in the tent." And He said, "I will certainly return to you according to the time of life, and behold, Sarah your wife shall have a son." (Sarah was listening in the tent door which was behind him.)"-Genesis 18:1-2, 9-10.

God gave Abraham and Sarah a specific time when their promised son will be born. He said next year by this time Sarah shall have a son. Sarah was ninety years!

Impossible made possible

When our hearts are towards the Lord, He shows Himself strong on our behalf for His glory. He makes the impossible possible! "And the LORD said to Abraham, "Why did Sarah laugh, saying, 'Shall I surely bear a child, since I am old?' Is anything too hard for the LORD? At the appointed time I will return to you, according to the time of life, and Sarah shall have a son.""-Genesis 18:13-14.

This was part of the test for both Abraham and Sarah. Sarah had to laugh, as this was impossible. At some points Abraham had to laugh too. The difference is that they did not doubt God. They were looking at the current situation of both being old. As part of the stages of the tests, God kept revealing Himself to them step by step all along the way. God asked them whether there was anything too hard for the LORD GOD ALMIGHTY? God said to Sarah I shall return to you and you shall have a son.

Ready: Vessel of honour

God fulfilled His promise and Sarah had a son in her old age, a miracle son. After years of waiting for this covenant miracle child, God asked Abraham to do something really strange. God was still testing Abraham as we read. This was the final test to confirm Abraham's faith in God as God pleased.

"Now it came to pass after these things that God tested Abraham, and said to him, "Abraham!" And he said, "Here I am." Then He said, "Take now your son, your only son Isaac, whom you love, and go to the land of Moriah, and offer him there as a burnt offering on one of the mountains of which I shall tell you.""-Genesis 22:1-2.

Abraham did not waste time. He obeyed immediately and the next morning set out to do as the Lord asked. At the place of sacrifice Abraham made some faith declaration worth studying. The son asked him the question that will break any good father's heart! "But Isaac spoke to Abraham his father and said, "My father!" And he said, "Here I am, my son." Then he said, "Look, the fire and the wood, but where is the lamb for a burnt offering?""-Genesis 22:7.

Abraham's response of faith
"And Abraham said, "My son, God will provide for Himself the lamb for a burnt offering." So the two of them went together."-Genesis 22:8.
Abraham had faith in God. He trusted God to come this far. If he was to kill this miracle child, he knew God was able to either raise him back or give them another miracle covenant child. He said to the son, God will provide a lamb for Himself.
Before they got to place of sacrifice, he informed his servants that the two of them will go

and worship and come back to them. "Then on the third day Abraham lifted his eyes and saw the place afar off. And Abraham said to his young men, "Stay here with the donkey; the lad and I will go yonder and worship, and we will come back to you.""-Genesis 22:4-5.

That was not what God said! God said go and sacrifice your only son. Was Abraham having the faith that even if he sacrificed Isaac, God was able to raise him up. He was trusting in the Creator of all things.

Final test

"And Abraham stretched out his hand and took the knife to slay his son."-Genesis 22:10. When God was still silent until the final stage for the actual sacrifice, Abraham did not hesitate. He went ahead and was about to finish the assignment when He was asked to stop. God can sometimes allow you to go through some trials that could even seem absolutely impossible and painful. Continue to trust Him to see you through at the end to see His goodness.

Divine response

"But the Angel of the LORD called to him from heaven and said, "Abraham, Abraham!" So he said, "Here I am." And He said, "Do not lay your hand on the lad, or do anything to him; **for now I know that you fear God,** since you have not withheld your son, your only son, from Me.""-Genesis 22:11-12.

In Abraham case, God was testing him on this 'Major,' Fear of God. If that were a degree it would be called just that. God said 'now I know that you fear God.' What do you think God is testing you on? Is it faith, trust or obedience to Him?

Divine provision

When the heart is right means trusting God completely will not be a problem. This is when God helps us when we trust Him completely. "Then Abraham lifted his eyes and looked, and there behind him was a ram caught in a thicket by its horns. So Abraham went and took the ram, and offered it up for a burnt offering instead of his son. And Abraham called the name of the place, The-LORD -Will-Provide; as it is said to this day, "In the Mount of the LORD it shall be provided.""-Genesis 22:13-14.

Vessel through all are blessed

". and said: "By Myself I have sworn, says the LORD, because you have done this thing, and have not withheld your son, your only son — blessing I will bless you, and multiplying I will multiply your descendants as the stars of the heaven and as the sand which is on the seashore; and your descendants shall possess the gate of their enemies. In your seed all the nations of the earth shall be blessed, because you have obeyed My voice.""-Genesis 22:16-18.

Now not only the families of the earth will be blessed but also the nations of the earth. Initially the blessings were for the families of the earth. "I will bless those who bless you, and I will curse him who curses you; and in you all the families of the earth shall be blessed.""-Genesis 12:3. Now God added you this range to involve nations just because of Abraham's fear of God. As there was no one greater than God, He swore by Himself to bless him this much.

Trusting God rewarded
"So Abraham returned to his young men, and they rose and went together to Beersheba; and Abraham dwelt at Beersheba."-Genesis 22:19.

This was what he said to the servants that they will come back to them after going to worship. That came to pass. Abraham demonstrated his love for God, respect, obedience, humility, reverence, obedience, faithfulness and summing it all into the fear of God. If you fear God you will do all that easily without effort.

4 Vessel for Deliverance

Who will lead?

Moses was born in Egypt at the time when the Israelites were enslaved by Pharaoh. This was a prophecy God gave Abraham with regards to his descendants becoming slaves for that period of time. God also said He was going to deliver them after the said period of time.

Moses grew up in the king's palace after a plan by her mum to protect him from being killed. When he grew up Moses discovered his root as part of the Israelite slaves. He tried to help them but that resulted in killing an Egyptian who was hitting an Israelite. Moses had to run away from Egypt as the king wanted to kill him.

God saw that his heart's desired was to save his brethren. He was a vessel that was ready and could be used. God had to come in and train him for the task. He had stayed at the palace as well and knew the protocol.

The call-The setup

Moses was living his life as a shepherd all these years in exile without any drama. Then all changed during an ordinary day going about his usual routine of taking the sheep to find pasture. "And the Angel of the LORD appeared to him in a flame of fire from the midst of a bush. So he looked, and behold, the bush was burning with fire, but the bush was not consumed. Then Moses said, "I will now turn aside and see this great sight, why the bush does not burn.""-Exodus 3:2-3.

Moses saw this amazing site and decided to investigate this phenomenon. How come the flames were not consuming the leaves? Out of a burning bush this voice called his name and a whole series of events began to unfold. "So when the LORD saw that he turned aside to look, God called to him from the midst of the bush and said, "Moses, Moses!" And he said, "Here I am." Then He said, "Do not draw near this place. Take your sandals off your feet, for the place where you stand is holy ground.""-Exodus 3:4-5.

Moses was about to start a journey and relationship with the Creator of the whole universe. He was about to introduce Himself to him as well as the details of his assignment.

Introduction of God

God went on to introduce Himself to Moses as the God of his fathers. "Moreover He said, "I am the God of your father—the God of Abraham, the God of Isaac, and the God of Jacob." And Moses hid his face, for he was afraid to look upon God."-Exodus 3:6.

The task

God went straight to the point. He was calling him to speak to Pharaoh to free His people. That would be possible if you are in a suicide mission!

"And the LORD said: "I have surely seen the oppression of My people who are in Egypt, and have heard their cry because of their taskmasters, for I know their sorrows. So I have come down to deliver them out of the hand of the Egyptians, and to bring them up from that land to a good and large land, to a land flowing with milk and honey, to the place of the Canaanites and the Hittites and the Amorites and the Perizzites and the Hivites and the Jebusites. Now therefore, behold, the cry of the children of Israel has come to Me, and I have also seen the oppression with which the Egyptians oppress them. Come now, therefore, and I will send you to Pharaoh that you may bring My people, the children of Israel, out of Egypt.""- Exodus 3:7-10.

Heart preparation

Moses run away from Egypt for fear of his life because of the incident. Moreover he looked at his current position and compared that to the task ahead. Who was he to speak to Pharaoh? They were not equals.

"But Moses said to God, "Who am I that I should go to Pharaoh, and that I should bring the children of Israel out of Egypt?" So He said, "I will certainly be with you. And this shall be a sign to you that I have sent you: When you have brought the people out of Egypt, you shall serve God on this mountain.""-Exodus 3:11-12.

Moses received the ultimate assurance that anyone can ever get on earth. That is for God to be with you. God said He will certainly be with him.

He was not going on his own. He has the backing of the King of kings.

Acceptance and planning

"Then Moses said to God, "Indeed, when I come to the children of Israel and say to them, 'The God of your fathers has sent me to you,' and they say to me, 'What is His name?' what shall I say to them?" And God said to Moses, "I AM WHO I AM." And He said, "Thus you shall say to the children of Israel, 'I AM has sent me to you.' ""-Exodus 3:13-14.

From this scripture you could see why God chose him. His heart was in the right place. Now Moses was asking operational questions that could rise up during the execution of this task. God provided all the necessary answers and strategies. "And I will give this people favor in the sight of the Egyptians; and it shall be, when you go, that you shall not go empty-handed. But every woman shall ask of her neighbor, namely, of her who dwells near her house, articles of silver, articles of gold, and clothing; and you shall put them on your sons and on your daughters. So you shall plunder the Egyptians.""-Exodus 3:21-22.

Vessel of honour

Beginning of supernatural unbelievable wonders!
"Then Moses answered and said, "But suppose they will not believe me or listen to my voice; suppose they say, 'The LORD has not appeared to you.' " So the LORD said to him, "What is that in your hand?" He said, "A rod." And He said, "Cast it on the ground." So he cast it on the ground, and it

became a serpent; and Moses fled from it. Then the LORD said to Moses, "Reach out your hand and take it by the tail" (and he reached out his hand and caught it, and it became a rod in his hand), "that they may believe that the LORD God of their fathers, the God of Abraham, the God of Isaac, and the God of Jacob, has appeared to you.""-Exodus 4:1-5.

Moses is now equipped with the presence of God backing him, the miracles he could show the children of Israel and the message to deliver to Pharaoh.

Used by God

"Then you shall say to Pharaoh, 'thus says the LORD: "Israel is My son, My firstborn. So I say to you, let My son go that he may serve Me. But if you refuse to let him go, indeed I will kill your son, your firstborn." ' ""-Exodus 4:22-23

God warned Moses that Pharaoh will not just allow them to go but will refuse.

Strengthened

God's plan may some times be seen as though all is failing and not going well. God works all things together for His good for us to His glory. It is mainly testing to see how much we trust Him. How much we can trust Him to the end until we see the outcome of His promises!

"So Moses returned to the LORD and said, "Lord, why have You brought trouble on this people? Why is it You have sent me? For since I came to Pharaoh to speak in Your name, he has done evil to this people; neither have You delivered Your people at all.""-Exodus 5:22-23.

Although Moses felt discouraged, God was not discouraged, as His plan never changes. "Then the LORD said to Moses, "Now you shall see what I will do to Pharaoh. For with a strong hand he will let them go, and with a strong hand he will drive them out of his land.""-Exodus 6:1.

We should try and have this attitude. When things seem not to go well we should remind ourselves that God will still make all things work together for our good at the end.

First born for first born

The end of the story was the warning God gave pharaoh concerning first borns. First-born sons are heirs to their Father's throne. It was very important and no one mess with people's first borns.

Three things God established

"And God spoke to Moses and said to him: "I am the LORD. I appeared to Abraham, to Isaac, and to Jacob, as God Almighty, but by My name LORD I was not known to them. I have also established My covenant with them, to give them the land of Canaan, the land of their pilgrimage, in which they were strangers."-Exodus 6:2-4.

God does not go back on His promises. He is a covenant maker and keeper. He made a covenant with Abraham, Isaac and Jacob to give them the land. Nothing was going to stop God from establishing that.

Secondly, He promised Abraham that after 400 years He will bring his descendants out of bondage. "And I have also heard the groaning of the children of Israel whom the Egyptians keep in bondage, and I have remembered My covenant."-Exodus 6:5.

God was going to get them out and rescue them from bondage. He was going to use all means possible to rescue them. "Therefore say to the children of Israel: 'I am the LORD; I will bring you out from under the burdens of the Egyptians, I will rescue you from their bondage, and I will redeem you with an outstretched arm and with great judgments."-Exodus 6:6.

There was going to be an established relationship between God and Israel. -"I will take you as My people, and I will be your God. Then you shall know that I am the LORD your God who brings you out from under the burdens of the Egyptians."-Exodus 6:7.

Vessel of honour final moment

After nine plagues God sent the tenth one about first borns He warned Pharaoh about. After the last plague, Moses and Israel were asked to leave Egypt immediately as God said. While they were leaving, Pharaoh changed his mind and sent his soldiers to recapture them.

Moses encouraged the people to hold their peace and see God's salvation "And Moses said to the people, "Do not be afraid. Stand still, and see the salvation of the LORD, which He will accomplish for you today. For the Egyptians whom you see today, you shall see again no more forever. The LORD will fight for you, and you shall hold your peace.""-Exodus 14:13-14.

God asked Moses to stop crying out to him and keep moving using the staff He gave his as the sceptre of his office. He asked him to stretch it over the Red Sea. "And the LORD said to Moses, "Why do you cry to Me? Tell the children of Israel to go forward. But lift up your rod, and stretch out your hand over the sea and divide it. And the children of Israel shall go on dry ground through the midst of the sea.

...And the Angel of God, who went before the camp of Israel, moved and went behind them; and the pillar of cloud went from before them and stood behind them. So it came between the camp of the Egyptians and the camp of Israel. Thus it was a cloud and darkness to the one, and it gave light by night to the other, so that the one did not come near the other all that night."-Exodus 14:15-16, 19-20.

God realised that the enemy army also come through the parted Red Sea with the aim to cause harm to His children. This was what God did to their chariots and their finally destination.

"And He took off their chariot wheels, so that they drove them with difficulty; and the Egyptians said, "Let us flee from the face of Israel, for the LORD fights for them against the Egyptians." Then the LORD said to Moses, "Stretch out your hand over the sea, that the waters may come back upon the Egyptians, on their chariots, and on their horsemen." And Moses stretched out his hand over the sea; and when the morning appeared, the sea returned to its full depth, while the Egyptians were fleeing into it. So the LORD overthrew the Egyptians in the midst of the sea. Then the waters returned and covered the chariots, the horsemen, and all the army of Pharaoh that came into the sea after them. Not so much as one of them remained."-Exodus 14:25-28.

Moses heart was right and he obeyed and trusted God. He was humble to work with a God and reverenced God.

5 Surrender of heart

Total obedience to God

King Hezekiah became king of Judah. He was 25 years old when he took on the reins. His heart was all for God. He followed the footsteps of King David and did what was right in the sight of God. He pleased God. "And he did what was right in the sight of the LORD, according to all that his father David had done."-II Kings 18:3.

The first act of obedience to God was to remove all the high places designated for idol worship. The children of Israel were even worshipping the bronze serpent as far back as Moses' time. They were burning incense to this image and called it *nehushtan.*

Heart of Hezekiah

Everyone has been given the same gift of free will to make choices in all areas of life. King Hezekiah chose to trust God Almighty consistently. He focused his life in seeking God's way by following Him and most importantly doing the will of God by obeying His commandments.

"He trusted in the LORD God of Israel, so that after him was none like him among all the kings of Judah, nor who were before him. For he held fast to the LORD; he did not depart from following Him, but kept His commandments, which the LORD had commanded Moses."-II Kings 18:5-6.

Hezekiah respected and loved God just as his great grandfather David did. This type of attitude was not going to be missed by God.

God's response

"The LORD was with him; he prospered wherever he went. And he rebelled against the king of Assyria and did not serve him."-II Kings 18:7. God was with him and was able to rebel against the king of Assyria.

Vessel of honour

Threat and blasphemy from the Assyrian king. "Then the Rabshakeh said to them, "Say now to Hezekiah, 'thus says the great king, the king of Assyria: "What confidence is this in which you trust? You speak of having plans and power for war; but they are mere words. And in whom do you trust, that you rebel against me?"-II Kings 18:19-20.

The king of Assyria made a grave error in blaspheming against God. He boasted that he has destroyed any nation he attacked and no gods were able to deliver them from his hand. He said the same about the God of Israel. "Who among all the gods of the lands have delivered their countries from my hand, that the LORD should deliver Jerusalem from my hand?' ""-II Kings 18:35. They did not answer this report according to the order of king Hezekiah.

Kings response

"And so it was, when King Hezekiah heard it, that he tore his clothes, covered himself with sackcloth, and went into the house of the LORD."-II Kings 19:1

He sent for the elders as well as the prophet. He declared the day as one of rebuke, blasphemy against God. They lifted up their voice to pray. Hezekiah did not call his army generals for war strategic planning meetings. He presented the case of blasphemy to the Almighty God.

The prophet sent word to the king. "And Isaiah said to them, "Thus you shall say to your master, 'Thus says the LORD: "Do not be afraid of the words which you have heard, with which the servants of the king of Assyria have blasphemed Me. Surely I will send a spirit upon him, and he shall hear a rumor and return to his own land; and I will cause him to fall by the sword in his own land." ' """-II Kings 19:6-7.

More threats more prayers

"And Hezekiah received the letter from the hand of the messengers, and read it; and Hezekiah went up to the house of the LORD, and spread it before the LORD. Then Hezekiah prayed before the LORD, and said: "O LORD God of Israel, the One who dwells between the cherubim, You are God, You alone, of all the kingdoms of the earth. You have made heaven and earth."
II Kings 19:14-15.

The heart of Hezekiah was towards God and that was his first call. He prayed to God first. This time he took the letter threatening the nation to God. The prophet was sent to deliver another message to king Hezekiah. "Then Isaiah the son of Amoz sent to Hezekiah, saying, "Thus says the LORD God of Israel: 'Because you have prayed to Me against Sennacherib king of Assyria, I have heard.'"-II Kings 19:20.

Wouldn't that be great to hear from God? This should teach us that once we fear God and doing His will He hears our prayers even at the time of extreme threat and possible annihilation.

God's response
God responded by preventing the enemy from entering Israel. The psalmist declared that God is our refuge and strength. Indeed He proved Himself so strong this king did not come near the nation at all. God defended the city for David and also for His own sake.

""Therefore thus says the LORD concerning the king of Assyria: 'He shall not come into this city, nor shoot an arrow there, nor come before it with shield, nor build a siege mound against it. By the way that he came, by the same shall he return; and he shall not come into this city,' Says the LORD. 'For I will defend this city, to save it For My own sake and for My servant David's sake.' ""-II Kings 19:32-34.

Action against blasphemy

"And it came to pass on a certain night that the angel of the LORD went out, and killed in the camp of the Assyrians one hundred and eighty-five thousand; and when people arose early in the morning, there were the corpses—all dead. So Sennacherib king of Assyria departed and went away, returned home, and remained at Nineveh."-II Kings 19:35-36.

The is the reason no one should mess with God because of His people. The king of Assyria insulted God because he was going to attack His people as he did with other nations. The other nations had idols that had no power. One angel who destroyed that many soldiers is simply unbelievable! That is the kind of God protecting you and me. His power speaks for itself.

Vessel of honour extended life

"In those days Hezekiah was sick and near death. And Isaiah the prophet, the son of Amoz, went to him and said to him, "Thus says the LORD: 'Set your house in order, for you shall die, and not live.' ""-II Kings 20:1.

After God delivered Hezekiah from his enemies, the Bible recorded that he became sick and was very serious. God asked him to put things in order as he was going to die. However, the king refused to accept this message.

He prayed to God presenting to Him how he has walked faithfully with the Lord. ""Remember now, O LORD, I pray, how I have walked before You in truth and with a loyal heart, and have done what was good in Your sight." And Hezekiah wept bitterly."-II Kings 20:3.

God heard his prayer and saw his tears. He was going to heal him and on top give him fifteen more years to live. ""Return and tell Hezekiah the leader of My people, 'Thus says the LORD, the God of David your father: "I have heard your prayer, I have seen your tears; surely I will heal you. On the third day you shall go up to the house of the LORD. And I will add to your days fifteen years. I will deliver you and this city from the hand of the king of Assyria; and I will defend this city for My own sake, and for the sake of My servant David." ' ""-II Kings 20:5-6.

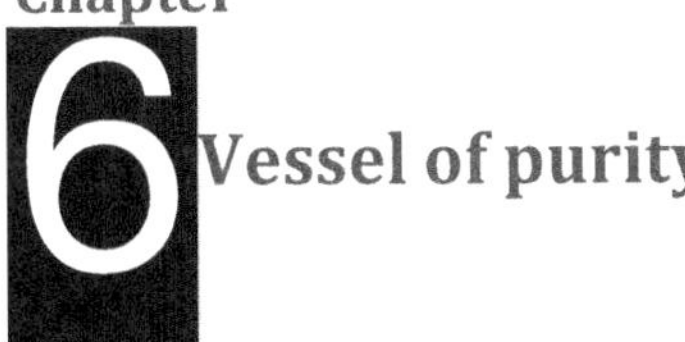

6 Vessel of purity

Young person chosen

When God wanted to fulfill His promise to Adam, He needed a vessel of honour ready for the task. An angel was sent to visit a young virgin called Mary.

"Now in the sixth month the angel Gabriel was sent by God to a city of Galilee named Nazareth, to a virgin betrothed to a man whose name was Joseph, of the house of David. The virgin's name was Mary. And having come in, the angel said to her, "Rejoice, highly favored one, the Lord is with you; blessed are you among women!""-Luke 1:26-28

After the initial greetings, the angel reassured Mary not to be afraid. He delivered the detailed message given to him by God to Mary. Mary found favour with God thus chosen to be part of God's plan to bring up the incarnate God.

"Then the angel said to her, "Do not be afraid, Mary, for you have found favor with God. And behold, you will conceive in your womb and bring forth a Son, and shall call His name JESUS. He will be great, and will be called the Son of the Highest; and the Lord God will give Him the throne of His father David. And He will reign over the house of

Jacob forever, and of His kingdom there will be no end.""-Luke 1:30-33.

 Mary's response: Initially Mary was thinking rationally and naturally, as all would have done. If I am going to have this baby then I need a man. Was that not how God planned from Adam and Eve's time? She was engaged to Joseph. "Then Mary said to the angel, "How can this be, since I do not know a man?""-Luke 1:34.

Divine order

"And the angel answered and said to her, " The Holy Spirit will come upon you, and the power of the Highest will overshadow you; therefore, also, that Holy One who is to be born will be called the Son of God."-Luke 1:35.

Mary's question was from a genuine heart seeking more clarification as she was already on board with the favour bestowed on her. That was why the angel took time to explain the supernatural involvement of the Holy Spirit in God's plan.

Vessel of honour at work

"Then Mary said, "Behold the maidservant of the Lord! Let it be to me according to your word." And the angel departed from her."-Luke 1:38

Mary was now clear on how this divine assignment was to proceed. She surrendered to the will of God as she had a heart that was ready for the Master's use. What a blessing!

 7 Holy Spirit's Temple

Ordinary made extraordinary

Vessels ready for the Master's use: The Bible teaches that our bodies are to be kept holy as they are the temple of the Holy Spirit. He comes to reside in us. "Or do you not know that your body is the temple of the Holy Spirit who is in you, whom you have from God, and you are not your own? For you were bought at a price; therefore glorify God in your body and in your spirit, which are God's."-I Corinthians 6:19-20.

The apostle Paul was teaching the church how important their lives were especially their bodies. This also applies to us. He explained that as followers of Jesus Christ, our bodies are the temples of the Holy Spirit.

The explanation here should be noted carefully. He said our body is for the Holy Spirit. The Holy Spirit is in you. The Holy Spirit you have is from God. That means our bodies are not for us with the reasons given in the same teaching. Our bodies are not our own because Jesus Christ bought our freedom at a price. He lost His life in the cross to pay for our sins and freedom to live and accepted as children of Almighty God.

In the same way we cannot use another person's property anyhow we want, we should do the same with the Holy Spirit's property, your body. Paul teaches us what we can do to please God in this. We are to glorify God in our body and our spirit, which are also both God's.

Treasure in earthen vessel

God does not go about looking for what society may describe as the greats! God rather looks for anyone whose heart is ready to receive Him. Those who receive the finished work of Jesus and accept Him as Saviour to forgive their sins and Lord to lead them become children of God. We may not have life all figured out or having all put together perfectly, but God sees our hearts. If our hearts are towards Him, God is able to perfect His plan in us.

God in turn puts His Holy Spirit in their hearts. We now have this ultimate divine treasure in our weak earthen vessels! "But we have this treasure in earthen vessels, that the excellence of the power may be of God and not of us."-II Corinthians 4:7.

Because of the presence of God's power in us, we are able to face all manners of trials and His Spirit keep us going. "We are hard-pressed on every side, yet not crushed; we are perplexed, but not in despair; persecuted, but not forsaken; struck down, but not destroyed— always carrying about in the body the dying of the Lord Jesus, that the life of Jesus also may be manifested in our body."-II Corinthians 4:8-10.

8 Instrument ready for Master's use

The heart of the persecutor

After Paul's conversion, he once gave a testimony of who he used to be and what he did. He was born to Jewish parent in Tarsus (in modern day Turkey). He was taught under an esteemed Pharisee called Gamaliel. Paul was taught according to the strictness of the father's law.

""I am indeed a Jew, born in Tarsus of Cilicia, but brought up in this city at the feet of Gamaliel, taught according to the strictness of our fathers' law, and was zealous toward God as you all are today."-Acts 22:3.

Paul who was called Saul (apparently his name was interchangeable) was zealous towards God. That meant persecuting the people known as the Way (followers of Christ) was the right thing to do. "I persecuted this Way to the death, binding and delivering into prisons both men and women, as also the high priest bears me witness, and all the council of the elders, from whom I also received letters to the brethren, and went to Damascus to bring in chains even those who were there to Jerusalem to be punished."-Acts 22:4-5.

His conversion

"Then Saul, still breathing threats and murder against the disciples of the Lord, went to the high priest and asked letters from him to the synagogues of Damascus, so that if he found any who were of the Way, whether men or women, he might bring them bound to Jerusalem."-Acts 9:1-2

It was an ordinary day with a religious zealot trying to save his religious stance by attempting to stop this new way. Saul was determined to bring these people bound to Jerusalem. He had written authority and backing from the high priest to execute this.

"As he journeyed he came near Damascus, and suddenly a light shone around him from heaven. Then he fell to the ground, and heard a voice saying to him, "Saul, Saul, why are you persecuting Me?""-Acts 9:3-4.

This can be seen as a very powerful encounter. Although Paul thought he was attacking and persecuting the followers of Jesus Christ, see what Jesus said to him. Jesus asked him why was he persecuting Him, the King of Kings and Lord of lords! The presence was so awesome and powerful that he fell from his horse to the ground! A light shone around him from heaven. What was Saul's response to the Lord?

"And he said, "Who are You, Lord?" -Acts 9:5a. Saul was asking who was talking to him. He was asking if he was the Lord. Jesus responded but first identifying Himself. "... Then the Lord said, "I am

Jesus, whom you are persecuting. It is hard for you to kick against the goads.""-Acts 9:5.

Indeed, it will be impossible to fight Jesus and win. God is a Warrior and have never lost any battle or war till date. Saul was now trembling on seeing the seriousness of his actions against Christians because of ignorance. "So he, trembling and astonished, said, "Lord, what do You want me to do?" Then the Lord said to him, "Arise and go into the city, and you will be told what you must do.""-Acts 9:6.

That was a heart ready for the Master's use. He asked the Lord what He wanted him to do. In other word he surrendered his will and heart to Jesus right away. He was ready to do whatever Jesus asked him to do. All what he had done against God was about to be forgiven. He was about to be ushered into the ministry of Jesus Christ through rigorous preparation. Jesus asked him to go to the city and will be told what to do.

"And the men who journeyed with him stood speechless, hearing a voice but seeing no one. Then Saul arose from the ground, and when his eyes were opened he saw no one. But they led him by the hand and brought him into Damascus. And he was three days without sight, and neither ate nor drank."-Acts 9:7-9.

Saul was temporarily blind. The powerful light of Jesus, which shone around him, might have caused that for a purpose.

Preparation process

The Lord came to a man called Ananias in a vision and gave him specific instructions regarding ministering to Saul. God directed him to where Saul could he found. "Now there was a certain disciple at Damascus named Ananias; and to him the Lord said in a vision, "Ananias." And he said, "Here I am, Lord." So the Lord said to him, "Arise and go to the street called Straight, and inquire at the house of Judas for one called Saul of Tarsus, for behold, he is praying."-Acts 9:10-11.

Ananias understood exactly what Jesus was saying to him. It was like a suicide mission! This Saul's reputation is well known among the Christians from the time he was consenting to the stoning and death of Stephen, a follower of Jesus Christ. Ananias discussed his concerns with the Lord: "Then Ananias answered, "Lord, I have heard from many about this man, how much harm he has done to Your saints in Jerusalem. And here he has authority from the chief priests to bind all who call on Your name.""-Acts 9:13-14.

"But the Lord said to him, "Go, for he is a chosen vessel of Mine to bear My name before Gentiles, kings, and the children of Israel. For I will show him how many things he must suffer for My name's sake.""-Acts 9:15-16.

See what Jesus said, he is a chosen vessel. He was to be prepared to be a vessel of honour to the Lord. His heart was right before God. His heart was seen as right when he surrendered to Him upon understanding the errors he was committing against Him.

On the other side where Saul was staying, God also gave him a vision. "And in a vision he has seen a man named Ananias coming in and putting his hand on him, so that he might receive his sight.""-Acts 9:12.

Ananias obeyed the Lord, overcame his fears and carried out the Lord's will. "And Ananias went his way and entered the house; and laying his hands on him he said, "Brother Saul, the Lord Jesus, who appeared to you on the road as you came, has sent me that you may receive your sight and be filled with the Holy Spirit.""-Acts 9:17.

Saul received his sight and had something to eat afterwards. He stayed in Damascus with the saints. The Christian people he planned to destroy at Damascus became his new family. "Immediately there fell from his eyes something like scales, and he received his sight at once; and he arose and was baptised. So when he had received food, he was strengthened. Then Saul spent some days with the disciples at Damascus."-Acts 9:18-19.

Vessels of honour

"Immediately he preached the Christ in the synagogues, that He is the Son of God."-Acts 9:20. Who else could preach better than Saul on this occasion? He was persecuting Jesus' followers all along until this supernatural encounter that caused him to totally surrender to Jesus. Now he has been filled with the Holy Spirit! What did they expect? There was going to be an explosion of the word of God from his testimony. Jesus is the Sin of God was Paul's theme for ministration.

Reaction

Your past: Some people influenced by the devil will not be allowed to see past your past!

"Then all who heard were amazed, and said, "Is this not he who destroyed those who called on this name in Jerusalem, and has come here for that purpose, so that he might bring them bound to the chief priests?""-Acts 9:21. Don't let that stop you from proclaiming the gospel of Jesus Christ.

Bolder for Christ

Paul understood what it took to fight for what one believed. He was doing so when he was a Pharisee persecuting the church. He was not going to bow down to persecution and threats. Instead he went on the 'offensive' and defended the faith. "But Saul increased all the more in strength, and confounded the Jews who dwelt in Damascus, proving that this Jesus is the Christ."-Acts 9:22.

We are to have this attitude to defend the faith that we have in Christ Jesus. We have the word of life and the testimony of Jesus Christ to share. We should not be stopped. We must be unstoppable!

Persecuting the vessel of honour

"Now after many days were past, the Jews plotted to kill him. But their plot became known. And they watched the gates day and night, to kill him. Then the disciples took him by night and let him down through the wall in a large basket."-Acts 9:23-25.

Paul was now at the other end of the persecution 'stick.' He learnt quickly how the presence of the Holy Spirit residing and empowering God's children attracts the wrath of Satan. In the same way that God uses human beings whose hearts gets transformed for Him, the same applies to how Satan will influence and use people. The Bible calls those He influences to plan attacks to physically harm God's children as wicked men and women.

King David experienced this wickedness and saw the deliverance of the Lord. "When the wicked came against me to eat up my flesh, my enemies and foes, they stumbled and fell." Psalms 27:2. God was David's light and salvation and he was delivered by Him.

The Christians protected Paul and helped him to escape after getting to know the evil murderous plot. All the negative views regarding Christians are not always true. Majority are genuinely loving and do look after one another all the time.

Vessel isolated, introduced and acceptance?
"And when Saul had come to Jerusalem, he tried to join the disciples; but they were all afraid of him, and did not believe that he was a disciple."-Acts 9:26.

Paul went back to Jerusalem after his conversation. While there he tried to join his new found family of believers in Christ Jesus. Initially the fear of his past records overcame some of the believers. That was unfortunate, but who could blame them? All was not lost. A man named Joseph and nicknamed Barnabas came to his rescue.

This man named Joseph was such a great encourager that he was known by his nickname rather than the real name. The name meant an encourager. The first time Barnabas was mentioned was when he led the way by selling his personal possession and laid the proceeds under the feet of the apostles. This was when the early church started.

On this occasion Barnabas courageously vouched for Paul when the church in Jerusalem were suspicious of this former persecutor of the church wishing to join them. "But Barnabas took him and brought him to the apostles. And he declared to them how he had seen the Lord on the road, and that He had spoken to him, and how he had preached boldly at Damascus in the name of Jesus. So he was with them at Jerusalem, coming in and going out."
Acts 9:27-28.

Escaped death
"And he spoke boldly in the name of the Lord Jesus and disputed against the Hellenists, but they attempted to kill him. When the brethren found out, they brought him down to Caesarea and sent him out to Tarsus."-Acts 9:29-30.

Paul continued to speak boldly in the name of the Lord Jesus Christ. Once again the Hellenistic that he disputed against tried to kill him. The brethren once again protected him as they did in the other town. They sent him to somewhere else.

Peace in the church
"Then the churches throughout all Judea, Galilee, and Samaria had peace and were edified. And walking in the fear of the Lord and in the comfort of the Holy Spirit, they were multiplied."-Acts 9:31

The ministry of Paul will take volumes of books to collate and teach. Paul was used mightily in his time than almost anyone else. He fulfilled his calling to the gentiles, and to appear before kings as God said.

Lesson/ encouragement:
Anyone who allows themselves to be used by the devil to persecute you in any way because of your lifestyle as a follower of Jesus Christ is actually persecuting the Jesus Christ. Jesus can fight His own battles as the King of Kings. He is able to deliver you and even call and use the persecutors into His work like Paul.

Also, the person who may be seen, as the persecutor could be the next great vessel or instrument God will use. Satan will attempt to destroy any vessel God uses. He tried several time to kill Paul right from the beginning. Notice that he had no death threats when he was persecuting the church.

Conclusion

God looks at the heart and test our minds. Let us demonstrate what David did to be called the man after God's heart. In our walk with God remember what we studied that made David a man after God's heart.

⊙ Love God

⊙ Reverence God

⊙ Obedience to God

⊙ Trusted God

⊙ Respect for God

⊙ Fear of God

⊙ Repentant

⊙ Faithful

⊙ Devoted

⊙ Humility

There are many more in the Bible such as we bearing the fruits of the Holy Spirit. "Gentleness, self-control. Against such there is no law."- Galatians 5:23

Reference

1. Edmonson, Rod. 10 Reasons David is called a man after God's heart. Bible Study tool. https://www.biblestudytools.com/blogs/ron-edmondson/10-reasons-david-is-called-a-man-after-god-s-own-heart.html. (Accessed 2Sep 3020).
2. Halloran, Kevin. 10 things to know about Barnabas. https://www.leadershipresources.org/who-is-barnabas-in-the-bible-10-things-to-know/